Belair Early Years Art

Rhona Whiteford

Acknowledgements

The author and the publishers would like to thank the following for their invaluable help and support during the preparation of this book:

- the staff and children of St David Haigh and Aspull CE Primary School, Headteacher Julie Charnley and class teacher Chris Charnock;

- the staff and children of St Oswald's Catholic Primary School, Headteacher Tony Brown and class teachers Joanne Cunliffe and Debbie Knott.

Published by Collins, An imprint of HarperCollins*Publishers*
77 – 85 Fulham Palace Road, Hammersmith, London, W6 8JB

Browse the complete Collins catalogue at
www.collinseducation.com

© HarperCollins*Publishers* Limited 2012
Previously published in 2007 by Folens
First published in 2001 by Belair Publications

10 9 8 7 6 5 4 3 2 1

ISBN-13 978-0-00-744793-0

Rhona Whiteford asserts her moral rights to be identified as the author of this work

MIX
Paper from
responsible sources
FSC
www.fsc.org
FSC™ C007454

British Library Cataloguing in Publication Data
A Catalogue record for this publication is available from the British Library

All Early learning goals, Areas of learning and development, and Aspects of learning quoted in this book are taken from the *Statutory Framework for the Early Years Foundation Stage*, Department for Education, 2012 (available at www.education.gov.uk/publications). This information is licensed under the terms of the Open Government Licence (www.nationalarchives.gov.uk/doc/open-government-licence).

Every effort has been made to trace copyright holders and to obtain their permission for the use of copyright material. The authors and publishers will gladly receive any information enabling them to rectify any error or omission in subsequent editions.

Cover concept: Mount Deluxe   Cover design: Linda Miles, Lodestone Publishing
Cover photography: Nigel Meager   Editor: Elizabeth Miles
Page layout: Jane Conway   Photography: Roger Brown and Kelvin Freeman

Extracts referred to in this book are:
'Yellow Butter, Purple Jelly' by Mary Ann Hoberman; *Can't You Sleep, Little Bear?* by Martin Waddell, published by Walker Books; 'I Know a Man Called Mr Red' (oral tradition), 'The North Wind Doth Blow' (oral tradition), 'A Chubby Little Snowman' by Elisabeth Matterson; all from *This Little Puffin*, published by Puffin Books. *Out and About* by Shirley Hughes, published by Walker Books and Lothrop, Lee & Shepard; *Peepo* by Janet and Allan Ahlberg, published by Puffin Books; 'Ten in a Bed' (oral tradition); *The Blue Balloon* by Mick inkpen, published by Hodder and Little Brown & Co; 'Water in Bottles' by Rodney Bennett and Clive Sansom from *Speech Rhymes*, published by A & C Black Limited; 'Who Made Footprints in the Snow?' by Tom Stainer, published by the BBC; *Lost in the Snow* by Ian Beck, published by Scholastic.

Printed and bound by Printing Express Limited, Hong Kong

Contents

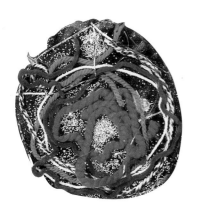

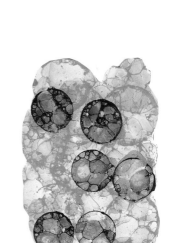

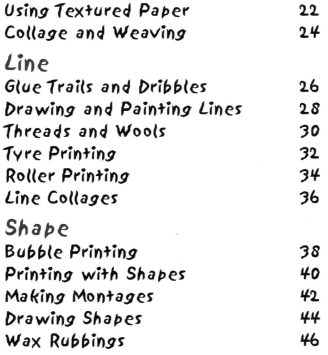

3

Introduction

The **Belair Early Years** series has been well-loved by early years educators working with the under-fives for many years. This re-launched edition of these practical resource books offers popular, tried and tested ideas, all written by professionals working in early years education. The inspirational ideas will support educators in delivering the three characteristics of effective teaching and learning identified in the Statutory Framework for the Early Years Foundation Stage 2012: playing and exploring, active learning, and creating and thinking critically.

The guiding principles at the heart of the EYFS Framework 2012 emphasise the importance of the unique child, the impact of positive relationships and enabling environments on children's learning and development, and that children develop and learn in different ways and at different rates. The 'hands on' activities in **Belair Early Years** fit this ethos perfectly and are ideal for developing the EYFS prime areas of learning (Communication and language, Physical development, Personal, social and emotional development) and specific areas of learning (Literacy, Mathematics, Understanding the world, Expressive arts and design) which should be implemented through a mix of child-initiated and adult-led activities. Purposeful play is vital for children's development, whether leading their own play or participating in play guided by adults.

Throughout this book full-colour photography is used to offer inspiration for presenting and developing children's individual work with creative display ideas for each theme. Display is highly beneficial as a stimulus for further exploration, as well as providing a visual communication of ideas and a creative record of children's learning journeys. In addition to descriptions of the activities, each theme in this book provides clear Learning Intentions and extension ideas and activities as Home Links to involve parents/carers in their child's learning.

This title, **Art**, particularly supports children's progress towards attaining the Early Learning Goals in Communication and language, Physical development and Personal, social and emotional development. It also provides opportunities to explore Understanding the world and, of course, Expressive arts and design.

Children relish the total body and mind experience involved in all types of art and the urge to create art can be ignited easily, yet last a lifetime. Yes, the processes can be taught, but the inspiration, creativity and enthusiasm can only be caught from the teacher. It's through art that we can show children how satisfying it is to produce something creative, expressive and aesthetically pleasing which can also be enjoyed by others. It's a soothing yet energising experience, inspires incredible conversation and can be a very positive individual, independent or a social event. It's the essence of active learning.

In an enabling environment, art can help develop play and exploration, foster creativity and critical thinking. For adults, anything goes in art – it's in the eye of the beholder so each young child's creative product is as worthy as another's – there are no labelled markers like the type of book one can read, the legibility of emergent writing, the ability to throw a ball. Everyone's work is personal, unique and satisfying and if children are shown how to appreciate that, then art can be a vital tool for personal, social and emotional development. And art is always so much fun.

I hope that adults and children alike will enjoy exploring the activities in this book.

Rhona Whiteford

Monoprints

Learning Intentions

- To become familiar with the names of colours and to describe them.

- To experience putting paint on paper by printing.

- To become aware of the feel and transferability of paint.

- To communicate thoughts and feelings to others.

Technique

- Cover the table with a plastic sheet or provide melamine boards for the children to work on. Provide assorted colours of ready-mix paint and small sheets of white paper.

- Ask the children to pick their favourite single paint colour. Squeeze a dessertspoonful of the paint on the table or board in front of each child.

- Ask the children to use their palms to spread the paint smoothly over an area, about 30 by 20 centimetres, and then to experiment with fingers to pull, push and draw any type of line design in the smooth surface.

- When a child is satisfied with a design, carefully place the paper over it and smooth the paper gently to fix the paint and produce a print. Lift the paper by the corners and dry flat.

There were 3 in the bed and the little one said...

Discussion Points

- Ask the children to name as many colours as they can. List them on the board. Which are the children's favourite colours?

- Encourage individual children to describe single colours by linking them to feelings. For example, ask: 'Is red a happy/cold/angry colour?' 'What items or events do individual colours remind you of?' (Examples: red/fire, blue/my best trainers, grey/a sad day.)

- Discuss and compare the textures of the paint, table and paper. Ask: 'Which of these feels slippery, smooth or rough?' 'Which feeling do you like best?'

- Discuss the movement of the paint and the children's fingers. Ask: 'What shapes and lines can you make if you move your finger slowly?' 'Are the shapes and lines different if you move your finger quickly?'

- Ask the children which parts of the activity they liked or disliked. Would they like to have another go?

Development Work

- Print onto coloured paper (see photograph right) and talk about the pairs of colours. Can both colours be seen or, for example, is yellow paint hidden when it is on yellow paper?

- Thoroughly mix equal amounts of two colours of paint on the table before printing onto white paper, to create a new, third colour. Talk about the new colour the children have made.

- Draw a definite design in the paint, such as a face, circles or straight lines.

- Read and discuss poems that use evocative colours, for example, 'Yellow Butter, Purple Jelly' by Mary Ann Hoberman. Cut out the appropriate coloured monoprints to go with the colours and foods mentioned in this poem. Display with the poem.

Can't you sleep, Little Bear?

Display

- Mount the monoprints as a border round an important poster or notice.

- Mount as a rainbow brick wall for the outside of your home corner house. This can then become a magic house or, perhaps, the Gingerbread House from *Hansel and Gretel*.

- Tessellate the prints to make a large patchwork quilt for Little Bear's bed from the story, *Can't You Sleep, Little Bear?* by Martin Waddell.

- Make bunting by hanging the prints in a row on coloured string across a wall.

- Make individual beds for the children's own drawings of themselves. Use a shoebox lid and fold a monoprint round it as a coverlet (see the photograph on page 5). Cut out the child's picture and slide it into the bed. Mount in a group, with a line from the song, 'There were ten in the beds and the little one said, "Roll over, roll over"'. Adjust the number to suit the number of items in your display.

Home Links

Ask parents or carers to:

- encourage their children to make colour choices when choosing what to wear after school

- ask their children's opinions about colours when decorating the home or choosing household items

- help their children sort toys into colour sets

- encourage their children to look at family hair and eye colours.

Finger Painting

Learning Intentions

- To learn about the feel of paint and to explore colour.

- To control paint by drawing with fingers.

- To become familiar with basic painting skills.

- To take turns.

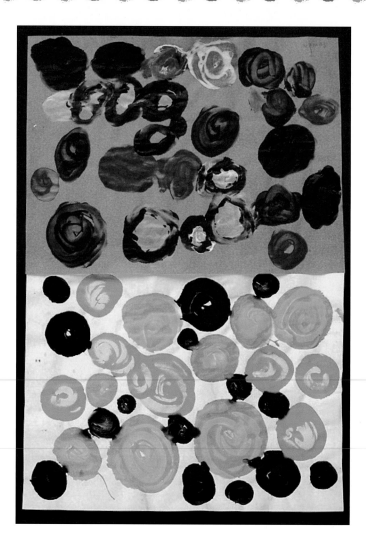

Technique

- Work in groups of three to four children, providing a palette of ready-mix paints for each child. Position it just above the children's paper so that paint does not have to be carried far.

- Show the children how to take turns to load a finger with an appropriate quantity of paint. Encourage them to draw tight curls, dots and open circles in a single colour to get a feel for the paint and to discover how to use it.

- Show the children basic skills (how to catch drips, wipe fingers and turn the paper as they work), reminding them to take care not to mix separate colours and not to overload their finger with paint.

- Explain that once the painting finger is dry and the line feint, it is time to dip the finger into the paint again.

Discussion Points

- Discuss ranges and shades of colour, such as red, pink, orange, apricot and yellow.

- Identify the shapes they are making, such curls, dots and circles. Ask: 'Is the circle open or filled in?'

- Talk about the feel of the paint. When they dip their finger in the paint, does it feel cold, warm, slippery, sticky?

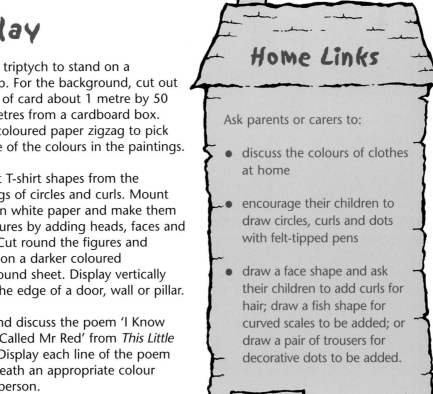

Development Work

- With the children working in pairs, ask them to use finger painting to draw a large round shape for a face, adding features and tight coloured curls (see the photograph on page 8). Use a wide palette of colours to give plenty of opportunities for choice and discussion.

- Provide the children with small pieces of paper and colour palettes, and ask them to draw a picture of their own. It can be any combination of line and colour, and their own interpretation of a subject.

Display

- Make a triptych to stand on a tabletop. For the background, cut out a piece of card about 1 metre by 50 centimetres from a cardboard box. Add a coloured paper zigzag to pick out one of the colours in the paintings.

- Cut out T-shirt shapes from the paintings of circles and curls. Mount these on white paper and make them into figures by adding heads, faces and limbs. Cut round the figures and mount on a darker coloured background sheet. Display vertically along the edge of a door, wall or pillar.

- Read and discuss the poem 'I Know a Man Called Mr Red' from *This Little Puffin*. Display each line of the poem underneath an appropriate colour T-shirt person.

Home Links

Ask parents or carers to:

- discuss the colours of clothes at home

- encourage their children to draw circles, curls and dots with felt-tipped pens

- draw a face shape and ask their children to add curls for hair; draw a fish shape for curved scales to be added; or draw a pair of trousers for decorative dots to be added.

Wet-paper Blends

Learning Intentions

- To discover the nature of powder paint and to know how it is changed by water.

- To find out how colours combine and how wet paper behaves.

- To communicate ideas, thoughts and feelings to others.

Technique

- Provide absorbent cartridge paper, water pots, paintbrushes or sponges, and dry powder paints.

- Show the children how to wet the paper (without drowning it!). Use long paintbrush strokes or a sponge. Let the water soak in for a minute.

- Ask the class to use a finger and thumb to sprinkle tiny amounts of dry powder paint onto the damp paper and watch as the paint is absorbed into the wet areas. Then ask them to draw an abstract track through the water and paint with a finger to blend some areas.

- Talk about the type of line the children are making. 'Is it curved, straight or spiral?' 'What new colours have been made as the paint combines?'

Discussion Points

- Identify the shades of colour produced as the colours merge. Talk about which colours are darker and which colours are lighter.

- Talk about how powder paint behaves when it comes into contact with water. Introduce the word 'dissolves'.

- Introduce other vocabulary, such as 'damp', 'brush-strokes', 'absorbent', 'soak', 'dry', 'sprinkle' and 'powder'.

Development Work

- Help the children to draw solid circles of water carefully so that the water lies on the surface of the paper and does not run. Drop a little powder paint in the centre of the circles. Watch it spread and mingle with the water. Allow to dry.

- Ask the children to use felt-tipped pens to draw pictures of themselves on white paper. Help the children to cut these out and mount them on each child's dry swirling painting to produce a picture of 'Me in a coloured mist'.

- Talk about other mists the children may have experienced, such as fog, a steamed-up bathroom, low cloud on a hillside or the coloured mist produced by fireworks on Bonfire Night, at Diwali, Chinese New Year or other festivals of light and fire. For young children to appreciate the connection, do this activity on a foggy day, after a small firework display or as part of work on a festival.

- Read and discuss poems on autumn and bonfires from *Out and About* by Shirley Hughes. List some of the colour and movement words used. Write one word on each child's wet-paper blend picture.

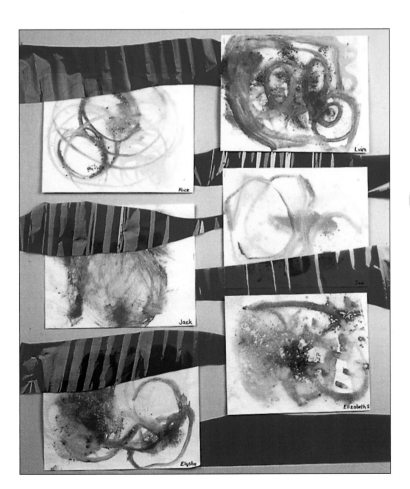

Display

- Ask groups of three or four children to do a wet-paper blend picture on a large piece of paper. This can be used as a background for the title of a festival or weather display. Write the title in black lettering with a coloured drop shadow for a three-dimensional effect.

- Mount groups of wet-paper blends on pastel shades of paper. Cover the edges of the display as shown with strips of coloured Cellophane to represent mist. Position the display near your weather board.

Marbling

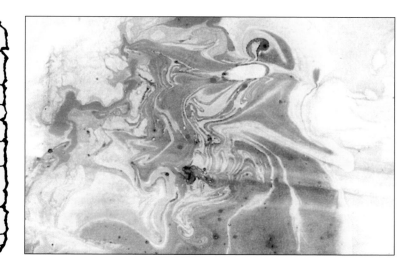

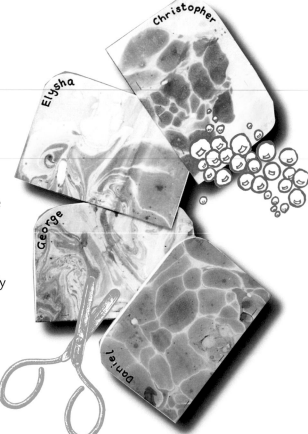

Technique

- Prepare a large drying area for the art work. Supply marbling inks in small, squeezy dropper-bottles. Fill a shallow tray with cold water to a depth of 3 centimetres. You will also need tweezers and a straw or long feather.

- Work in groups of about four children. Drop coin-size blobs of colour onto the water's surface using two or three colours. Watch as they combine.

- Use a long feather or straw to gently pull paint around the surface. This needs a delicate touch, just on the surface.

- When the children are happy with the paint pattern, lay a sheet of paper gently on the surface. Wait a few seconds until the paper begins to darken with moisture, then gently lift it up from one corner using tweezers. Continue to lift the paper with a peeling-back motion. Lay it flat to dry.

- The surface of the water should be fairly empty and can either be cleaned off with a piece of paper or more colour can be added for the next print.

Discussion Points

- Name the colours used and any new colours that emerged from blending, such as green (a mix of blue and yellow).

- Encourage the children to describe the lines and shapes they create, using words such as 'wavy', 'long', 'curved', 'swirling', 'twirling', 'blob', 'patch' and 'feathered'.

- Talk about the way the paint moves on the water. Ask: 'Is the paint moving on its own on the surface?' 'Does it move slowly or quickly?'

Development Work

- Use coloured paper and see which colours of paint are hidden and which show up on the background colour.

- Thoroughly mix the paint and water to see what happens to the colours and the resulting print.

- To demonstrate that the marbling inks work because they float, try this experiment. Drop a little ready-mix water-based paint onto the surface and watch it sink to the bottom. See if you can make a print with this. Next, drop a spoonful of cooking oil on the surface and see it float. Point out how the oil floats. Mix a little paint with oil and see if this floats like the inks.

- Use the finished marble prints as covers for small notebooks. Place a marbled sheet face down and three sheets of plain paper of the same size on top. Fold in half, so that the marbled sheet is on the outside. Staple near the spine and round off the corners with scissors (see the photograph on page 12).

- Learn the song, 'One two three four five, once I saw a fish alive' and talk about how fish move underwater. Then read any traditional story about ducks, such as *The Ugly Duckling*. Compare the fish with the ducks – pointing out that the ducks float on the surface, like the paint.

Display

- Use blue- and green-based marble prints to represent water in a large wall picture, or as rainbow puddles for a rainy day picture.

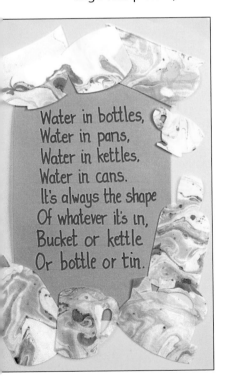

Water in bottles,
Water in pans,
Water in kettles,
Water in cans.
It's always the shape
Of whatever it's in,
Bucket or kettle
Or bottle or tin.

- Cut out large leaf shapes from the prints to make a giant's beanstalk to accompany work on *Jack and the Beanstalk* or a similar story. Attach to a stem made with green tissue paper wound round a length of wire and add a child's drawing of the Giant.

- Experiment with water to see how it fits into the shape of its container. Record this by using marbled sheets cut into different shaped containers, such as bottles, bowls and cups.

- Read and display the poem, 'Water in Bottles' by Rodney Bennett and Clive Sansom. Attach the marble print cut-out containers around the poem.

Home Links

Ask parents or carers to:

- encourage their children to experiment with different containers in the bath to learn about the behaviour of water

- let their children help with any cooking or baking that requires mixing colours, such as adding food colours or adding jam to rice pudding.

13

Mixing Shades and Colours

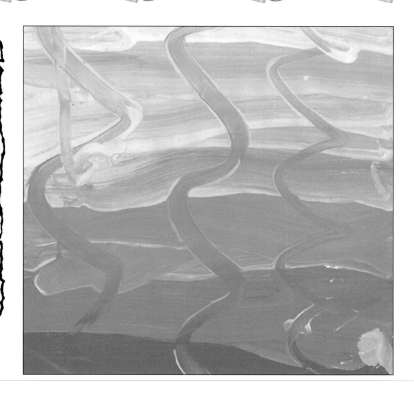

Technique

- Provide assorted colours of ready-mix paint (extra white), different sized paintbrushes, palettes and paper.

- Help the children to put two large spoonfuls of white paint in a palette. Add only a tiny amount of one chosen colour to the white and mix this to produce a pale shade. Paint this in a wide stripe onto the paper, starting at one end. Show the children how to do straight brushstrokes, bending the bristles.

- Add extra tiny amounts of the chosen colour, one blob at a time, and continue by painting darker stripes until the paper is covered. Add some decoration with a wiggly finger-line across the stripes.

I saw three ships go sailing by...

Discussion Points

- Talk about the names of colours and shades, such as 'light', 'pale' and dark'. Use comparative adjectives, such as 'lighter' and 'darker'.

- Discuss the behaviour of colours as more pigment is added. Ask the children whether the change is to a lighter or a darker shade. Can they think of other items that are the same shades of colour?

- Talk about items that are dark and things that are light, for example day, night, under spotlights, shadowy corners and contrasting colours on clothes.

Development Work

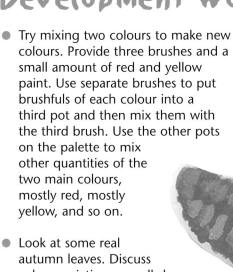

- Try mixing two colours to make new colours. Provide three brushes and a small amount of red and yellow paint. Use separate brushes to put brushfuls of each colour into a third pot and then mix them with the third brush. Use the other pots on the palette to mix other quantities of the two main colours, mostly red, mostly yellow, and so on.

- Look at some real autumn leaves. Discuss colour variation, overall shapes, the veins and the edges.

- Paint a leaf on tracing paper using the mixed red, orange and yellow shades. Allow to dry and then cut out the leaf shapes and mount on a window to allow the light to shine through the paper.

- Make up names for shades of colour, as on colour shade cards from hardware stores. Encourage the children to be imaginative, perhaps using memories as inspiration. For example, 'This colour is like my dog. I'll call it "Blotchy Brown"'.

Display

- Arrange the painted leaves into a huge sunflower, as shown. Staple the points of the leaves where they meet and cover the centre with two paper fans joined to form a circle.

- Cut the longest side of the striped, shaded paintings into a zigzag and mount them together horizontally as a border around other work.

- Cut out large letters, numerals or shapes from the striped paintings.

- Use the stripes to make collage sections of larger pictures, such as boats to illustrate a traditional song (see the photograph on page 14).

Home Links

Ask parents or carers to:

- help their children learn shades of colours when picking clothes or looking for household items

- play 'I-spy a shade of colour' with their children

- take their children to a hardware store and help them read the names of the many shades of paints.

Multimedia Colour

Learning Intentions

- To know that the colour remains the same whatever the medium.

- To understand that each medium behaves differently and makes its own line.

- To respect the ideas of others.

- To develop creative independence.

Technique

- Provide assorted colours and sizes of felt-tipped pens, ballpoint pens, chalks, wax crayons, pencil crayons and ready-mix paints.

- Encourage the children to paint whatever they like on the paper but they must use each of the media they are given and stick to one colour only.

- Ask them to fill the page with any shapes, lines, marks or blobs they wish, leaving no space untouched.

Discussion Points

- Discuss the behaviour of the different media. 'Was it slippery, rough, thin, thick, wet, dry, greasy?'

- Discuss the different types of lines and shapes. Introduce words such as 'thick', 'thin', 'wavy', 'jagged', 'looped', 'long' and 'short'.

- Ask the children why they picked their colour. 'Why is it your favourite?' 'What does it make you think of?'

- Look at and discuss everyone's work, encouraging positive comments only.

- How did the children decide when their work was finished? Were they satisfied with the effect?

Development Work

- Give each child the same colour of paper and media. Talk about whether the results are successful.

- See how the different media behave on a textured surface, such as plain, textured non-vinyl wallpaper.

- Draw a person using the different media to represent specific features. For example, use a ballpoint pen for hair and pastels for skin tones.

- Ask the children to choose their favourite medium and use a similarly free style of painting. This time the children can use as many colours as they wish. Why did they choose the medium they did? What do they like about it?

- Compare the single-medium paintings with the multimedia paintings. Which do they like best? Why?

- Look at paintings by professional artists that use different media, such as watercolour and oil paintings. Which do the children like best, and why?

Display

- Make giant coloured sweets using a single colour of mixed media work on white paper for each. Place the sheets in a row but bend them to form half-cylindrical shapes. Staple in place and add different shades of tissue-paper twists to each end. Mount each child's work on a background colour that will flatter the piece.

- Have a 'Painting of the week' spot where one child each week has a piece of work on show. Cover the back of an easel with clean paper and mount the painting there with a label saying 'This week's artist'.

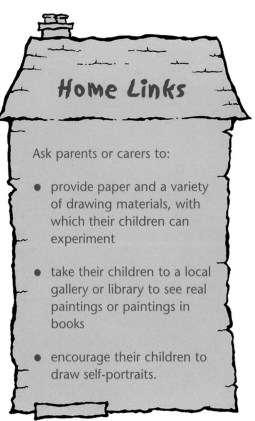

Home Links

Ask parents or carers to:

- provide paper and a variety of drawing materials, with which their children can experiment

- take their children to a local gallery or library to see real paintings or paintings in books

- encourage their children to draw self-portraits.

Textured Paintings

Learning Intentions

- To understand that textured paint can be made by adding different materials to smooth paint.

- To understand that different materials create different textures.

- To use new words to describe various textures.

Technique

- Provide the children with assorted colours of ready-mix paint, large mixing pots, assorted brushes, glue spreaders, PVA glue, painting trowels and a variety of materials that can be mixed with paint to create textures, such as sawdust, washing powder, crushed leaves, straw and rice.

- Half-fill mixing pots with a chosen colour of paint, then add the same quantity of a textured material, such as sawdust. Add a tablespoon of PVA glue to help the material adhere to the paint when dry. Mix well and add more paint or material depending on the density required.

- Try adding just glue to the paint. This will make the paint dry with a plastic sheen.

- Ask the children to experiment with the textures by creating an abstract composition that covers the whole paper, leaving no spaces. Encourage them to try out various application tools, such as painting trowels, glue spreaders and strips of cardboard.

Discussion Points

- Talk about what we mean by 'texture'. Discuss favourite textures and those the children hate. 'Do you like sticky textures?' 'Do you like the feel of fabrics such as velvet?'

- Introduce vocabulary such as 'rough', 'smooth', 'knobbly', 'soft', 'silky', 'sticky' and 'hard'.

- Ask the children whether the textures make the paint behave differently. 'Is it easier to paint with the glue mixture?' 'Can the paint mixture be piled up and shaped?' 'Can straight lines be drawn with a textured finish?'

Development Work

- Paint snowmen with a mix of white washing powder and white ready-mix paint. Sprinkle glitter on the wet paint and add features, such as hat and buttons, with pearlised paint.

- Paint a human or animal face and use grass or hay in paint for the hair or fur.

- Look at poems and songs about snow, such as 'The North Wind Doth Blow' and 'A Chubby Little Snowman' from *This Little Puffin*, and 'Who Made Footprints in the Snow?' by Tom Stanier.

Display

- To display the snowmen, mount on lilac or blue circles of card. Add small cut-out paper snowflakes and hang on strips of textured paper.

- To display abstract works, choose a mount which brings out the best colour in the piece. Mount a single piece of work with no other embellishments.

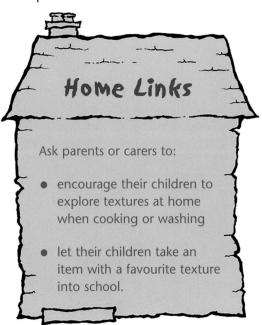

Home Links

Ask parents or carers to:

- encourage their children to explore textures at home when cooking or washing

- let their children take an item with a favourite texture into school.

Glue-printing Textures

Learning Intentions

- To make a print and to add a raised texture to it.

- To develop skills in using different materials and tools.

- To extend knowledge of texture and design.

Technique

- Provide coloured paper (metallic is particularly effective), glitter or coloured art sand, a rubber-based contact glue, and pastry-cutters or plastic open shapes. (This printing technique relies on the consistency of the rubber glue which holds its shape and does not run.)

- Set up two distinct areas on a table, the first for gluing and the second for glittering. Put glue in one saucer and the glitter or sand in another.

- Ask the children to choose a simple design, such as a row of star shapes. Show them how to dip a pastry-cutter or shape into the glue and then to place it carefully, glue-side down, onto the paper. Repeat this until the design is complete, taking care not to smudge the glue.

- Move the paper carefully to the glitter area, putting the paper onto a clean sheet to catch any excess glitter. Demonstrate how to sprinkle a heavy covering of glitter onto the glued areas, taking care to cover all the glue. When the glue is covered, lift the paper gently from one edge and let any excess glitter drop off onto the sheet below. Allow the glittery design to dry.

Development Work

- Use the same technique but with two colours of glitter. Wait a few minutes for the first glitter to dry, then repeat the process by printing more glue shapes onto the paper. These could overlap some of the first. Cover the glue with the second colour of glitter. Try soap powder or a duller coloured sand for the second print.

- Use the glittery prints to edge a painting or a greetings card.

- Make an abstract design using two printing shapes and powder paints in two colours. Print a first glue shape and dust with the first colour, then print with the second shape and add the second colour. Spray with a pastel fixative.

- Bake some biscuits, make cornflake cakes and a jelly and have a 'Tasting the texture party'. 'What do these feel like in your mouth?'

Display

- Print shapes on thin strips of paper and use as a border round a painting, poster or label.

- Print silver stars on gold paper for the front of a Christmas card.

- Mount abstract designs on plain paper to emphasise the textured, raised nature of the print.

Discussion Points

- Discuss the idea of a texture being the 'feel' of something. What are the children's favourite textures? Can they explain why?

- Talk about textures in the activity, such as that of the glue (slippery, sticky, dry, wet) and the glitter (hard, prickly, crunchy, rough). Think of other items that are similar to glue (honey) and glitter (sand, salt).

- Observe how the glue holds its shape and how the printing shape transfers the glue to the paper. Ask the children why the glitter sticks to the glue but not to the paper. Introduce vocabulary such as 'adhesive', 'hold', 'stick' and 'non-run'.

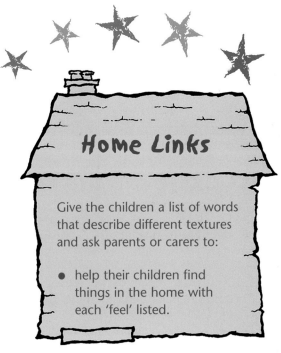

Home Links

Give the children a list of words that describe different textures and ask parents or carers to:

- help their children find things in the home with each 'feel' listed.

Using Textured Paper

Technique

- Ask the children to draw on textured paper with chalk. Provide them with paper cut into circles, rectangles or squares big enough for them to do sweeping, bold movements with their chalk.

- Show them how to draw with chalk, either with its tip or on its longest edge, to get a wide band of softer, dusty colour. Experiment by going over one patch more than once to make it bolder or by smudging a line with a finger to make it indistinct.

- Try using ready-mix paints on various types of paper, including tracing paper and heavily embossed, waterproof wallpaper pieces.

- Allow the children to paint whatever they like – for example, a cat, self-portrait or an abstract piece – and to observe the effect of the different textures of the paper on their brushes and painting style.

Discussion Points

- Can the children think of words to describe the texture of the chalk? Introduce words such as 'drag', 'dusty', 'dry', 'soft', 'light', 'delicate', 'powdery', 'misty' and 'smooth'.

- Discuss the differences between the texture of chalk and that of paint. 'How did the paint behave on the different surfaces?' 'Did it run off the surface, fall into cavities or soak in?' 'Did the texture of the paper make a difference to the style of the children's paintings?'

Development Work

- Try using pastels and oil pastels on smooth paper to see how they work. Compare the results with those of the chalk drawings.

- Encourage the children to draw on the playground or a section of pavement with large chalks. Ask pairs of children to work together and give each pair a restricted working area.

- Try painting directly onto a window using ready-mix paint. (Its future removal will be easier if a little PVA glue is added to the paint.) Try painting giant flowers, snowflakes or curtains.

- Look at the texture of an oil painting. Can the children see the brush strokes?

Home Links

Ask parents or carers to:

- bring in samples and roll-ends of plain wallpapers which can be painted on or used as backing paper for displaying other art work

- take their children on a walk round their home to look at the texture of the surfaces, such as the walls, floors and kitchen worktops. Which of these areas has a smooth surface?

Display

- Display the children's work alongside labels with trigger words for the children to discuss.

- Use a selection of textured papers to create a picture, as shown on page 22. Decorate each section with chalks, pastels or paints, and include other textured features, such as scrunched tissue paper for grass, and gathered, twisted crêpe paper for clouds.

- Hang tracing paper paintings in front of windows, using crêpe paper strips for decorative borders. Hang an odd number together at different heights so that the edges of each can be seen as shadows behind others.

Collage and Weaving

Learning Intentions

- To combine difficult and delicate materials to create new textures.

- To understand that a new texture can be made from others.

- To learn how to weave.

Technique

- Provide each child with a sheet of cardboard about 20 by 30 centimetres, foil, assorted colours of tissue paper, coloured Cellophane, and PVA glue.

- Tear pieces of foil large enough to cover the cardboard. Paste a thin layer of glue all over the board, lay the foil onto this and fold any excess over to the back. Any creases in the foil will add texture to the finished piece. Roughly tear tissue paper and coloured Cellophane into small, palm-sized pieces. Paste glue thinly over most of the foil and lay the tissue paper and Cellophane on top in an abstract pattern, allowing pieces to overlap. Allow to dry thoroughly.

Weaving Technique

- Provide assorted coloured papers and linear scrap materials (feathers, straws, wool and ribbon) to make a collage.

- Cut a coloured backing sheet to 25 by 15 centimetres and cut zigzags at one end to mark it as the top. Lay double-sided tape along the top and bottom of the backing sheet. Cut five thin 'warp' strips in a single colour and lay down evenly to overlap the tape. Tear or cut some strips for the 'weft'.

- Start at the top, weaving over and under an uneven number of warp strips. Ask the children to work down the sheet towards them and push each weft line upwards to touch the last one and so produce a tight weave.

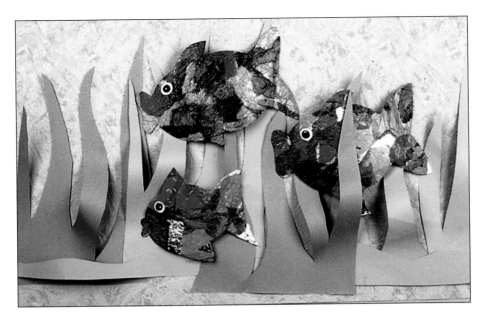

Discussion Points

- While working on the collage, discuss the shape and feel of the different materials and the way the colours mix to produce new shades and blends.

- Introduce vocabulary to describe the paper collage, such as 'creased', 'crinkled', 'shiny', 'delicate', 'fine' and 'transparent'.

- Use the correct technical vocabulary when weaving (weave, thread, warp, weft).

- Ask the children about items that are woven and list them: fabrics, mats, rugs, baskets, fencing, and so on.

Development Work

- Make fish-shaped paper collages. Create an abstract or wavy pattern on a square and, when dry, cut out simple fish shapes.

- Enjoy the nursery rhyme 'One, two, three, four, five, once I caught a fish alive' with the children.

- Create a paper face collage by placing the tissue pieces over the foil in a face shape. Add facial features.

- Weave using only two colours, one for the warp and one for the weft.

- Use wallpaper strips for the warp and thick woollen threads for the weft to introduce the idea of woven fabric.

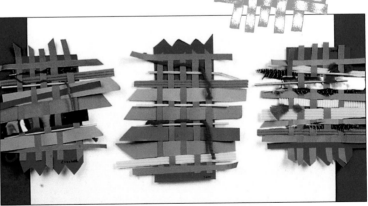

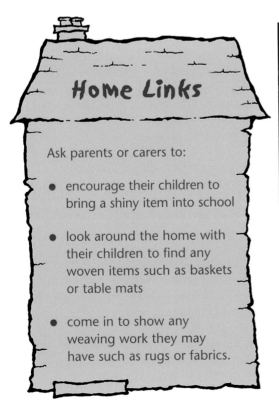

Home Links

Ask parents or carers to:

- encourage their children to bring a shiny item into school

- look around the home with their children to find any woven items such as baskets or table mats

- come in to show any weaving work they may have such as rugs or fabrics.

Display

- Display the paper collage fish on a blue background (see Development Work). Curve the fish outwards for a three-dimensional effect and staple on green paper strips for weeds.

- Mount the children's weavings on white backing paper but make sure the loose ends of the weft are secured at the back with double-sided tape or contact adhesive.

Glue Trails and Dribbles

Learning Intentions

- To know that lines can be made on paper without pencils or brushes.

- To experiment with a new medium.

- To use a range of appropriate vocabulary to describe the process of making abstract images.

Technique

- Provide white cartridge paper cut into dinner-plate sized pieces, PVA glue, glue spreaders, and six colours of dry powder paint.

- Working in twos or threes, ask the children to stir the glue until it has the consistency of syrup. (If the glue is cold or old you may need to add a tiny drop of water.)

- Gather glue onto a spreader and then allow it to dribble onto a circle of cartridge paper. Move your hand around to create a line, otherwise large blobs will collect. Before the paper is too heavily loaded with glue, take small pinches of a chosen colour of powder paint and sprinkle it over the surface. Continue until the paper is covered with a thin layer of the powder.

- Allow the glue to dry and absorb the paint, before tipping the excess powder onto newspaper.

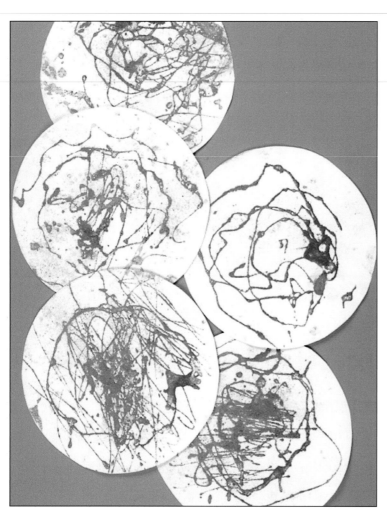

Discussion Points

- Discuss the process with the children as they work and encourage the use of appropriate vocabulary (such as dribble, trickle, drip, blob, fall, line, wave, thin, thick, sticky, tacky, light, heavy, powdery, dusty, scatter, sprinkle, shake and tap).

- Discuss the methods used by individual children. Are they making spirals, moving the glue from side to side, or creating splashes, drips or heaps?

- Discuss what the glue looks and feels like when it is wet and when it is dry. Compare these features with those of other liquids.

- Discuss how each child wanted their piece to look. Did they have an idea or did the work just evolve?

Development Work

- Dip a spoon in a pot of runny honey or golden syrup and show the children the trail the liquid makes. Draw a 'trail' picture – can the children tell you what it is?

- Look at the way raised line patterns are used for decorative purposes, such as on pottery, tiles, T-shirt motifs, vinyl and wallpapers.

- Make decorated candle cards for Christmas, Diwali or other festivals of light. Decorate a rectangle of coloured paper with glue dribbles, sprinkled with glitter. Glue a marbled-paper flame (see page 12) just behind the top of the candle.

- Use the technique to make tall, wild hair. Draw a face, cut it out and then mount it on a backing sheet. Use the dribbled glue technique to draw the hair and then sprinkle on glitter.

Display

- Mount several abstract works of the same colour on a matching coloured background.

- Create a free-standing display with the candle cards by taping a card roll behind each of them.

Home Links

Send a simple recipe home and ask parents or carers to:

- help their children follow the recipe and bake biscuits using syrup or honey.

Drawing and Painting Lines

Technique

- Begin with a variety of simple drawing tools, such as felt-tipped pens (broad and fine), pencils, crayons, chalks and pastels.

- Demonstrate a selection of line possibilities: straight, wavy, zigzag, thick, thin, feint, bold, curled, crenellated, slashed and crossed (see photograph below).

- Encourage the children to experiment and take the line from left to right on a sheet of paper, using all the space. Practise drawing patterns with a variety of different coloured lines only.

- For a large-scale group activity roll out about 3 metres of non-waterproof wallpaper on the floor and fasten down the ends. Use decorators' paintbrushes, rollers and pens to draw coloured, 3-metre-long lines down the paper. Start off with lines going from top to bottom, then change direction. Add felt-tipped pen lines. (See photograph above.)

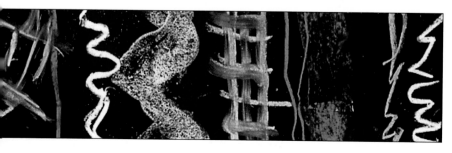

Discussion Points

- Talk about the shapes of lines and how much space they take up, for example a zigzag will cover more space than a straight line even if they are of the same thickness.

- Encourage the use of appropriate vocabulary (straight, wavy, thick, thin, medium, wobbly and zigzag).

- Talk about the practical organisation of the large group activity. 'How can you best avoid tripping up or stepping on the paper?' 'Where should the paint trays be put?'

- During the group activity talk about the length of the long lines compared to the children themselves. When the painting is dry see how many children can lie head to toe along a line.

- Talk about the thickness and texture of the lines produced by the rollers, paintbrushes and pens.

Development Work

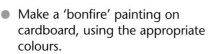

- Encourage the children to draw a border around a picture, using a variety of shapes or lines, such as tiny circles or a wavy line.

- Paint and draw lines in any direction and across each other to produce an abstract design.

- Make a 'bonfire' painting on cardboard, using the appropriate colours.

- Look at line drawings by famous artists such as L S Lowry (1887–1976).

- Make a display of fabrics with linear designs.

- Walk round your school looking for long lines, for example drainpipes, roads, curtains, paths, wallpaper, fences and lines on playgrounds.

- Look for lines in the wider environment, such as roads, footpaths, railway lines and road markings.

Display

- Mount a distinctive line drawing on plain paper in a special place and entitle it, 'Drawing of the week'. You could base the selection on general excellence or major progress.

- Mount a row of drawings on the same background and display along a tall edge, such as the side of a door or under a window sill, to emphasise the linear theme.

- Fold cardboard paintings in two places to display as a free-standing triptych, as with this Bonfire Night picture.

Home Links

Ask parents or carers to:

- encourage their children to record lines in a sketchbook and to bring it into school as a resource

- play an 'I-spy a ... line' game in which their children must find thick and thin lines when they are out and about. Who can find the most unusual ones?

Threads and Wools

Learning Intentions

- To understand that a line can be created with hard materials.

- To make structures with materials that are linear and flexible.

- To create lines using three-dimensional materials.

Techniques

- Create a circular wool and thread trail by covering a circle of thick paper or card with plenty of glue. Select threads from an assortment of wools, glitter ribbons, cottons and strings, and place them in the glue in any position. Help the children to cut the threads to the required lengths, if necessary. Finish off with a liberal dusting of glitter or coloured sand.

- Make an 'icy branch' thread hanging by spraying a twig with silver paint. Choose about six items from assorted white and silver strips (foil, wool, thread, ribbons, fabric strips) and glue them to the twig. Add other decorations, such as a feather, a star, a sequin or the child's name on a paper bird. Tie a length of white wool to the top for hanging.

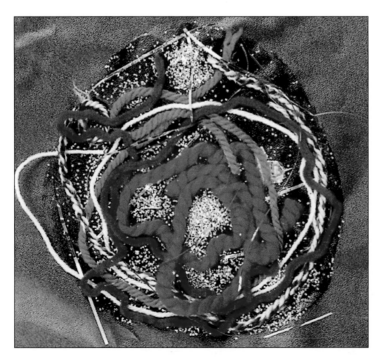

Discussion Points

- Talk about the flexibility of threads and what shapes can be made with them as lines. What do they feel like compared to drawn lines?

- Introduce appropriate vocabulary (such as fix, position, straight, bent, curved, wavy, coiled, wiggle, shiny, shimmering, dull, rough, smooth).

- Talk about the behaviour of the hanging threads. Do they move in the air or hang heavily? Do they catch the light?

- Describe the different threads and strips. 'Are they shiny/shimmering/dull/rough/wavy?'

Development Work

- Make hangings using single colours of wool and thread beads onto the end of each piece.

- Use matching coloured wool to tie round small toys and interesting items such as pine cones, corks, metal washers or old keys. Hang on threads of different lengths from a twig or a dowel.

- Make a display of small items that are circular and have lines as part of their design, for example rush table mats, baskets, wheels from toy cars, small bike wheels and saucers with coloured borders.

- Read winter stories, and talk about weather conditions and freezing ice. For example, read *Winnie in Winter* by Korky Paul and Valerie Thomas and look at the icicles on Winnie's house.

Display

- Display the circular thread trails as abstract lollipops. Make the sticks by tightly rolling coloured art paper, then attach the top of each stick to the back of a circle with adhesive tape. Push the lollipop handles into a tin of sand or florists' foam. Hide the tins behind paper fans, which can be taped to the table and the sticks.

- Suspend hangings in front of a window at different heights so that they catch the light.

Home Links

Ask parents or carers to:

- encourage their children to make line patterns on a circular piece of paper using lines of different colour, thickness and shape

- let their children help to defrost the freezer

- help their children find icicles in the winter.

31

Tyre Printing

Learning Intentions

- To understand that lines can be made on paper without pens or brushes.

- To discover that prints can be rolled onto a surface.

- To experiment with space and shape.

- To be able to describe actions.

Technique

- This is a fun printing activity that involves making lines with wheeled toys, such as small cars and tractors. You will also need sponges, assorted ready-mix paints and coloured art paper cut to different shapes.

- Squeeze a dessertspoonful of each colour of paint onto different plates. Spread the paints evenly over sponges.

- Choose a sheet of paper of any shape. Run a vehicle over a sponge several times until the wheels are well coated with paint, then 'drive it' over the paper in any direction.

- Use one vehicle for each colour but let the children experiment with direction, crossing lines, and trying different vehicles and colours of paint.

- Smaller vehicles can be driven in curves and arcs but larger ones will produce straight lines over a short distance.

- Explore the shape of the paper used by asking the children to start their print by driving from one corner outwards, then across the paper horizontally, then vertically, then diagonally, and finally in any direction.

Discussion Points

- Discuss how the lines look on the different shapes of paper. 'How many ways can a circle be cut by straight lines?' 'What about a rectangle?'

- Encourage the children to talk about each stage of the process. Look at the prints and ask: 'Did you drive the car in a line or a circle?'

- Discuss the patterns made by the tyres. What shapes can be seen? (Zigzags? Waves? Squares?)

- Ask: 'Which vehicles can draw curved lines?' 'Which can only draw straight lines?' Can the children draw a curved line with a big car on a larger sheet of paper?

Development Work

- Introduce the children to repeated patterns by encouraging them to print stripes in two, then three colours.

- Use the technique to draw parts of a large class picture. For example, grass can be painted with assorted vehicles and two to three green shades of paint. If the paint is not too wet, the painting can be done straight onto paper on a wall.

- Use the technique to paint hair, straw, thatched roofs, hairy bears or tassels on a magic carpet.

- Read *Lost in the Snow* by Ian Beck. Talk about how tracks and trails are made. Make footprints in a sandtray with dolls and action figures. Look for aircraft trails in the sky.

Display

- Make a repeated pattern out of the printed shapes, for example: rectangle, circle, rectangle, circle. Mount red circles on black paper and black rectangles on red paper, and so on. Display these in vertical or horizontal lines.

- Cover a sheet of paper with two colours of abstract tyre printing to use as a background for mounting smaller drawings.

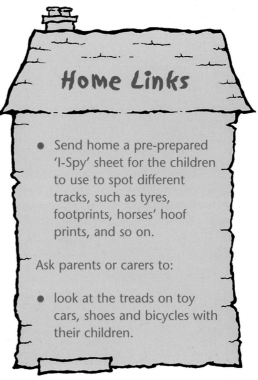

Home Links

- Send home a pre-prepared 'I-Spy' sheet for the children to use to spot different tracks, such as tyres, footprints, horses' hoof prints, and so on.

Ask parents or carers to:

- look at the treads on toy cars, shoes and bicycles with their children.

Roller Printing

Learning Intentions

- To understand how lines can be made on paper without pens or brushes.

- To use new vocabulary to describe a process.

Technique

- This is a fun, kinetic type of printing that is quick to do. Children enjoy watching it, so although it is done by one child at a time, several can be involved.

- Put three colours of ready-mix paint in separate pots. Provide a small rectangular tray with an edge, three large marbles, three teaspoons and assorted coloured paper, sized to fill the tray.

- Put a marble in each of the paints. Place the chosen paper in the tray and use a teaspoon to put a paint-covered marble onto the paper. Then tip the tray slightly from side to side, forwards and backwards. Watch the marble paint lines as it goes. You can put all three in at once or reload with one colour only.

Discussion Points

- Discuss the texture of the paint and how it clings to the marble and then prints an image as it rolls.

- Discuss the shapes of the lines and how the artist controls their direction.

- Encourage the use of appropriate vocabulary during the process (roll, rush, slow, fast, movement, direction, line, curve, knobbly, smooth, colours, cross, tip, lift).

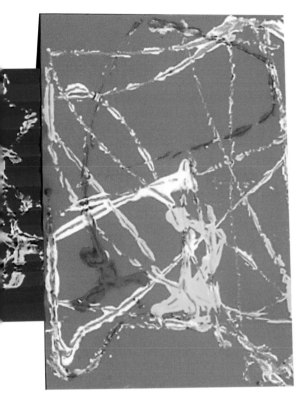

Development Work

● Create an overlay texture on top of a dry version of the main activity. Use PVA glue as the 'paint' for this overlay. Mix it with water to the consistency of the paint, then make tracks with the glue. Finally, sprinkle glitter on the wet glue. Wait for this to dry slightly and then tap off the excess.

● Play outside on bikes when there are puddles and look at the patterns made by the wet wheels. Roll balls of different sizes through the puddles.

● If possible, substitute small balls for the marbles and roll them across large sheets of paper placed on the floor or in a large, empty, sand tray.

● Look at water trails on windows, caused by condensation or rain. Which way do the trails go?

Display

● Mount the prints on black backgrounds to highlight the many colours. Display as a wave by arching out each sheet and then joining them in a continuous row.

● Use a glittered example to make into a Christmas card by folding the print in half and adding a large silver star on the front.

● Make into a cracker decoration by rolling a print into a cylinder and adding bunches of crêpe paper at each end, secured with fast-drying glue.

● Tape lots of prints together to cover a large card roll, such as a carpet roll. Stand up as a totem pole as shown in the photograph.

● Concertina-fold a print so that the direction of the lines is altered.

Home Links

Ask parents or carers to:

● play tenpin bowling with their children, using empty plastic bottles as pins

● play 'I-spy tracks', encouraging their children to notice the trails left by aircraft, slugs and wet tyres.

Line Collages

Learning Intentions

- To build images with three-dimensional lines.

- To consider the directions and appearance of three-dimensional lines.

- To develop skills in using scissors and glue.

Technique

- Provide assorted strips of paper, card, ribbon, wool and fabric, PVA glue, scissors and corrugated backing card.

- Ask the children to choose a selection of different strips to place crossways over the lines in the cardboard.

- Encourage the children to use a different material and shape of line each time. Tear materials into lines, cut them with shaped scissors, or cut them into larger waves or zigzags. Tightly twist tissue paper into an interesting 'thread' and use clear Cellophane to make an almost invisible line that shimmers.

- Help the children to cut pieces to the required size. Alternatively, leave some strips to hang over the edge to give a runaway effect.

- When the children are satisfied with the appearance of their collage, take off one piece at a time and dab a little glue along the space on the card. Then re-mount the strip. Start at the top and work downwards.

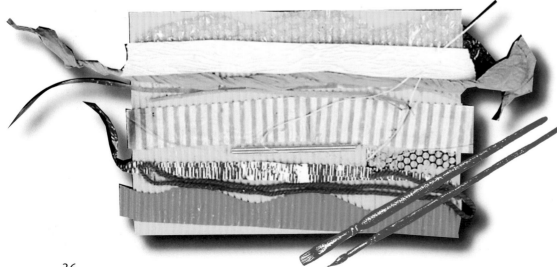

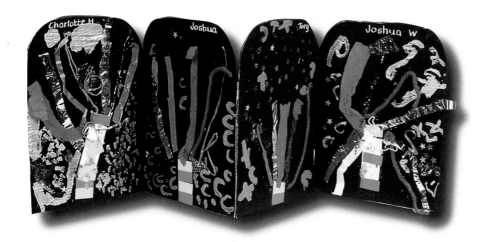

Discussion Points

- Talk about each person's choice of materials, colours, shapes and textures. Do they like the effect of textured lines crossing the corrugated ones? Would it look as good if they all went in the same direction?

- Encourage the use of appropriate vocabulary (cut, stick, position, line, texture, transparent, feel, direction).

Development Work

- Use the technique to make collages of fireworks for Bonfire Night or other festivals of light. Add explosions and crackles with dabs of pearlised paint and glitter-glue pens.

- Use the technique to make a mock weave. Glue a row of strips onto a backing piece, but leave the same size gap between each. Then add an evenly-spaced top row, going across as in a weave but gluing lightly instead.

- Read and discuss the poem 'Fire' by Shirley Hughes. Read and discuss stories about fire and light festivals, such as Diwali and Chinese New Year.

Display

- To make a free-standing zigzag of the fireworks collages, cut the top edges into a curve to add interest and then tape the sides together at the back to make a concertina shape.

- Display the collages free-standing by taping card rolls to the back. Alternatively, place a strip of tape from the left to the right side of the reverse, pulling it shorter than the actual length to bend the picture in an arc so that it will stand up. Display two or three collages against a toning drape of cloth.

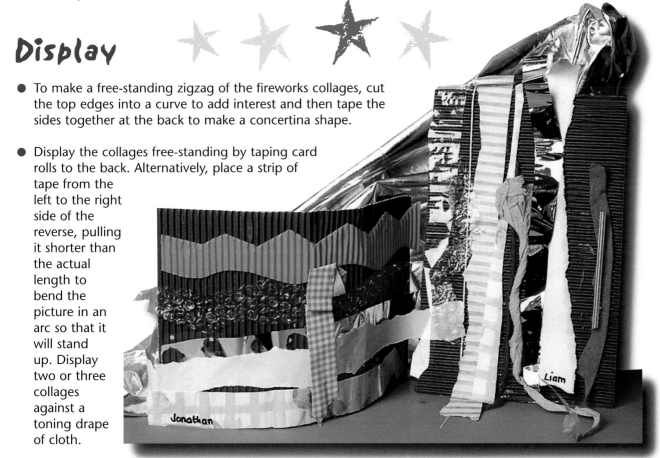

Bubble Printing

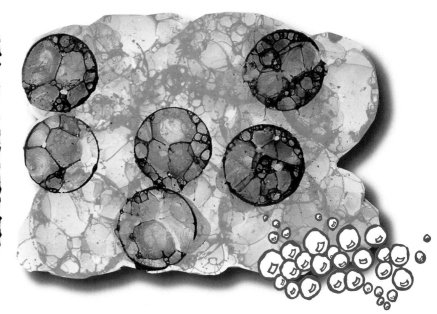

Learning Intentions

- To learn how to make a careful print using a delicate 'print block'.

- To learn about circular shapes and how they can be made into an image.

Technique

- Provide ready-mix paints, washing-up liquid, water, a shallow container, large plastic straws, paintbrushes and sheets of white paper, about 30 by 20 centimetres in size. Half-fill a mixing pot with paint and a half-teaspoon of washing-up liquid. Mix well and, if necessary, add one extra teaspoon of water at a time to produce a consistency that will blow into bubbles easily.

- Ask the children to each use a straw to blow into the mixture and produce a surface of coloured bubbles (make sure they blow, not suck!). Mix a selection of colours and encourage the children to enjoy blowing bubbles in each.

- To make a print, hold the outside edges of the paper over the bubbles, keeping it level and straight. Lower the paper vertically down to touch the top of the mixing pot, bursting the bubbles on the way. These bubbles burst onto the paper to make the print. The action should be gentle but firm.

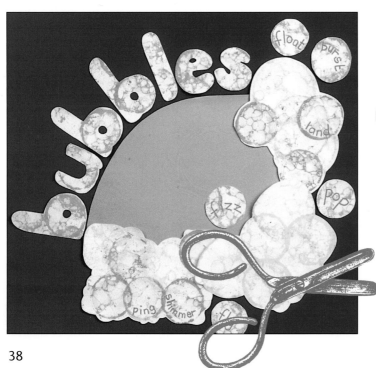

- To achieve a striking image cover the paper with a base bubble print, and then wait until it is dry before superimposing two or more single bubbles in a darker colour.

Discussion Points

- Discuss the fun of blowing bubbles. Have the children blown bubbles before?

- Discuss how the bubbles pop onto the paper, leaving a darker ring with a blotchy centre. Talk about the sizes, shapes and colours of the bubbles.

- Encourage the use of appropriate vocabulary (pop, burst, print, colour, shades, pale, dark, round, circle, lower, down, higher, straight).

Development Work

● Compare the technique with other printing techniques. Most rely on a printing block being pressed onto the paper, but here the paper is lowered onto the 'block'.

● Make bubble chicks or other birds by printing two circles side by side or slightly overlapping. Allow the print to dry and then use felt-tipped pens to draw eyes, beaks and legs. Alternatively, use coloured paper triangles as beaks.

● To make bubble hair, paint large faces on white paper, omitting the hair. When dry, add the hair with bubble prints by holding the paper so that the top of the head is lowered onto the bubbles. While one child holds the paper, another can bend down and guide it into position.

● Use a rectangular mixing pot to see if rectangular bubbles can be blown. 'Are bubbles always spherical?' If possible, test some of the wire bubble-making shapes that are available in a variety of geometric shapes.

● Teach the children the song, 'I'm Forever Blowing Bubbles'.

Display

● Make a frieze to display several birds or chicks. Cover a large piece of card with coloured backing paper and fold the card into a triptych with the centre facing outwards. Add zigzag strips of green art paper to the bottom for grass and stick the chicks or birds on top. Add other features, such as a sun or trees.

● Display the chicks or birds as free-standing objects by gluing a small card tube or hinge shape to the reverse or by making them into greetings cards.

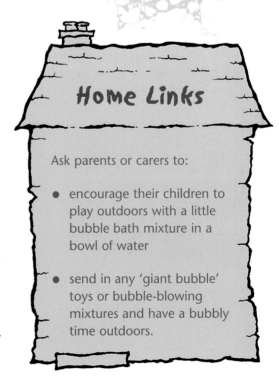

Home Links

Ask parents or carers to:

● encourage their children to play outdoors with a little bubble bath mixture in a bowl of water

● send in any 'giant bubble' toys or bubble-blowing mixtures and have a bubbly time outdoors.

Printing with Shapes

Learning Intentions

- To make simple prints with closed and open shapes.

- To use shapes to create images and designs.

Technique

- Provide the outside covers of large and small matchboxes, card tubes in various sizes, ready-mix paints (brown, blue and white) and art paper (brown, black, silver and orange). Restrict the number of printing shapes so that the children can concentrate on the shapes, how they are formed and how they tessellate.

- Put a centimetre-depth of each colour of paint in saucers. Place a rectangle and a circle shape next to each saucer. Encourage the children to put these back at the side of the correct colour so that the paints are not corrupted.

- Ask the children to dip a shape in the paint and check that it is not dripping off – they should wipe any excess on the edge of the saucer. Then carefully place the shape, edge vertically down, onto the paper. Slow, careful movements give good results. Use a second shape and colour to build up a pattern.

Discussion Points

- Discuss everyone's choice of colour and positioning of the shapes.

- Discuss how well the two shapes tessellate with themselves and each other.

- Use appropriate vocabulary (straight, corner, curve, sides, long, short, large, small, fit, match).

Development Work

- Go for a walk to look for rectangles and circles which are alone or in repeated patterns, for example in paths or walls.

- Sing 'Humpty Dumpty sat on a wall', and then look at Humpty Dumpty pictures and discuss the wall patterns.

- Experiment with the direction of the printing shapes. For example, print the rectangles with the bottom corners touching in a fan shape or superimpose the circles in a staggered order to give the impression of a spring.

- Make repeating patterns using the two shapes and two colours.

- Create pictures of faces, houses, figures or trees using the given shapes.

- Experiment with the blocks to change the shape that is printed. Try dabbing, twisting and streaking (see right). Print with part of a shape to create part of the image.

- Use other solid printing shapes, such as wooden blocks or polystyrene alphabet bath toys. Glue a handle to the reverse of these. The alphabet blocks can be used to print the children's names (see photograph on page 40).

Display

- Display a small selection of prints on an unusual textured background, such rush matting, hessian, a brick wall or wooden trellis. The texture will enhance the shape of the images.

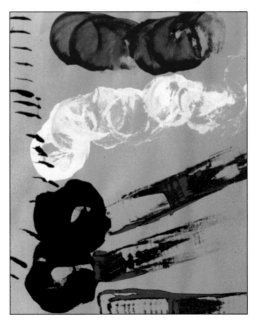

Making Montages

Technique

- Provide assorted dry leaves (pressed if possible), various natural items (rice, lentils, hay, feathers, shells, sand, cork, twigs), silver glitter, scraps of beige cardboard, grey paper, embossed white wallpaper and PVA glue.

- Encourage the children to rearrange a choice of natural materials on a sheet of grey paper until they are happy with the result. They could create an abstract work (collage) or an image (montage), such as a face, animal or bird.

- Pick one piece up from the final arrangement, apply a little glue to the back and then replace it on the backing. Continue in this way until the work is complete.

- For more powdery items apply the glue to the required place on the montage, then scatter the material thickly over it, tapping off the excess later.

Discussion Points

- Talk about the shapes, colours and textures. Let the children discover that non-geometric shapes are more difficult to describe. Encourage the use of appropriate vocabulary (curve, pointed, long, thin, wavy, round and jagged).

- Discuss how individual shapes can be used as part of the whole, asking for example: 'Is this useful for a wing?' or 'Would this shape fit into this space?'

Development Work

- See what kind of image can be made using just one material at a time, for example just twigs, dried peas, leaves or shells.

- Make a montage using fabrics of different kinds. Cut some fabrics into different-sized pieces and into regular and irregular shapes. Encourage the children to cut small items themselves while you hold the pieces taut.

- Display adult-made montages, such as dried-flower pictures, appliqué work, patchwork cushion covers and quilts, and montage motifs on children's clothes. Discuss the techniques used.

Display

- Make a border for each picture using strips of white embossed wallpaper. Glue strips round the edge and cut across the corners to complete the frame.

- Make a free-standing, three-dimensional mount by covering long, thin boxes with a complementary coloured art paper. Fix two or three montages to the box stands using double-sided adhesive tape.

- Single pictures can be displayed upright, supported by a triangular prism shape made of scrap card or a cardboard tube.

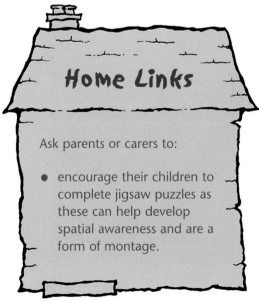

Home Links

Ask parents or carers to:

- encourage their children to complete jigsaw puzzles as these can help develop spatial awareness and are a form of montage.

Drawing Shapes

Technique

- Provide the children with various sizes of white and coloured paper and a selection of drawing media, such as chalks, charcoal, pastels, wax crayons, felt-tipped pens, oil pastels and hard and soft pencils. Encourage frequent drawing practise with a variety of media.

- Give each drawing time a clear purpose. For example, demonstrate how to use a new medium by drawing a variety of shapes and lines. Encourage the children to use the medium to draw representations of real or imaginary items.

- Use people or toys for life-drawing sessions. Scrutinise faces of friends or teddy bears at close quarters to see details and match them on the paper. Point out that the eyes are halfway down the face and level with the tops of the ears.

- Ask the children to look at and describe the shape of features and then to show you the shape on paper. Help the children as necessary, for example if they describe the edges of the eyes as pointed then show them how to make a point.

Discussion Points

- Discuss what the children can actually see. For example, ask: 'Do the arms come from the body at the bottom or at the top near the neck?'

- Ask the children to say what they can see and to then point to the appropriate place on their drawing. For example, 'Can you see a blue line near the Sun' or 'Does the sky seem to go behind the houses and all over the space?'

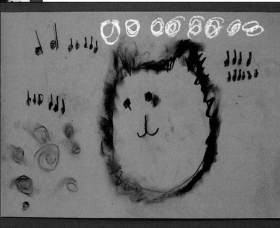

- Talk about the items they can see in terms of shape. For example, ask: 'Is the mouth a thin line or an open shape?', 'Are nostrils round, oval or slits?' or 'What shapes can you see in this cat/wall/house?'

Development Work

● Use pencils of different thickness and hardness. Show the children how to make thick soft lines by holding the pencil almost flat to the paper.

● Use chalks, pastels and charcoal for a powdery texture. Lines can be blurred by rubbing with a finger. Hold these media sideways for a wide pale line.

● Give the children a single colour of chalk, such as black. Ask them to complete atmospheric drawings, such as those on page 44 showing 'Monsters in a dark mist in the night!'

● Look at pencil drawings in popular stories such as *Winnie the Pooh* or *Tales of Beatrix Potter*. Do the children think they are effective?

● Look at and discuss the styles of drawings in a variety of favourite story books. Can they spot strong shapes in the illustrations?

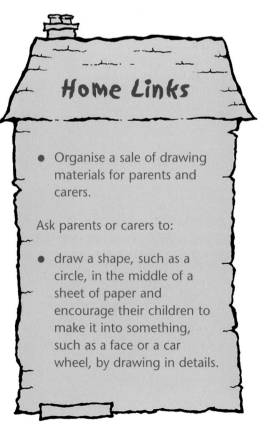

Home Links

● Organise a sale of drawing materials for parents and carers.

Ask parents or carers to:

● draw a shape, such as a circle, in the middle of a sheet of paper and encourage their children to make it into something, such as a face or a car wheel, by drawing in details.

Display

● Supply different shaped paper to draw on, such as circles, squares or rectangles, and mount these on similar shapes.

● Mount pictures singly, in pairs, threes or small groups as shown above. Vary the colour of the backing paper to draw attention to the group.

● Hang mounted drawings on thick strips of crêpe paper from the ceiling in groups of odd numbers.

● Mount a group of drawings at the end of a corridor so that people can focus on the display as they approach.

Wax Rubbings

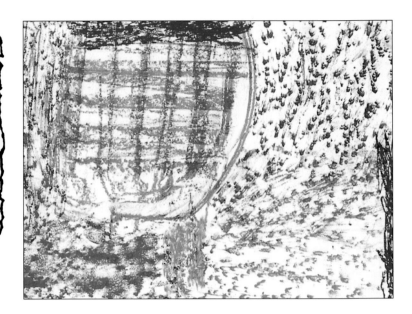

Technique

- Provide a selection of wax crayons and sheets of white paper.

- Ask the children to look for surfaces around them that show shapes clearly in relief, such as tiled floors, drain covers, construction bricks, house bricks, metal treads on steps and textured wall tiles.

- Place a sheet of paper onto a chosen surface. Remove any paper wrapping from the wax crayon and then, holding it on its side, rub the crayon across the paper away from the body in smooth, firm, slow strokes.

- Show the children how to place the paper directly over a shape they want to capture. Allow several attempts to get a good image. Encourage them to try using two or three colours over the same image.

- Remind them to always keep the paper still and press down hard with the crayons.

Discussion Points

- Discuss how the wax is transferred onto the paper.

- Point out that wax is brittle when cold and pliable when warm. Talk about the difference.

- See if the class can identify the shapes in individual wax rubbings.

- Look at and discuss the colours made by using two or three different wax crayons on top of each other.

Development Work

● Make a rubbings picture. Cut out assorted shapes from thin card and stick them onto a backing sheet of stiffer card. (The shapes can overlap or not, as you wish.) Put a clean sheet of white paper over the top to make a rubbing of this image. Repeat, using a new piece of paper and a different colour of wax.

● Vary the colour of the paper, perhaps using black paper with a strong white crayon or grey paper with a black crayon.

● Help the children to give the rubbings a paint wash. Mix a pale colour of ready-mix paint. Then, using firm, even strokes from left to right, brush the paint over the rubbing. Experiment with one colour of wax for the rubbing and a contrasting wash, or use multicolour wax and a weak black wash.

Display

● Display the rubbings as an abstract, as shown below, with a little natural decoration to contrast with the sharper lines of the rubbings.

● Mount the same rubbings pattern completed in different colours as a patchwork effect or in a single line along a work surface or beside a door.

● Use brick or tile rubbings to decorate the walls of a play house or to make the walls of the third little pig's house in the story, *The Three Little Pigs*.

● Use cut out rubbings of round items for sweets on the walls of the witch's house from *Hansel and Gretel*.

Home Links

Ask parents or carers to:

● bring in unwanted wall tiles with a relief texture (mount these on a flat surface so the children can feel the shape of the edges and the texture of the surfaces)

● take their children round the house to feel the relief on items such as wall tiles.

Large and Small Spaces

Technique

● Provide each child with a selection of coloured chalks and a large sheet of paper to work on. Introduce the idea of space by asking them to design whole-page patterns to fill the space, by drawing a selection of line shapes across the page from left to right, such as squiggles, stripes, crosses, dots and zigzags. (Some children might find it easier if an adult begins each line of pattern for the child to finish off.)

● Ask each child to draw a small picture of him or herself, filling a piece of paper about 10 by 15 centimetres. Cut it out and mount on a large piece of paper, painted to represent a beach or field.

● Cut paper to fit the inside base of a large, empty matchbox. Show the children a completed picture on this size of paper and discuss the contents of what the child will draw. Encourage them to fill all the tiny space with colour and detail using pencil crayons. Glue the finished picture to the back of the matchbox.

Discussion Points

● Talk about the big and small pictures using appropriate vocabulary (large, huge, giant, massive, small, little, tiny, minute).

● Introduce adjectives of comparison, such as 'larger', 'smaller' and 'biggest'.

● Discuss the items you could fit into a tiny matchbox or a large field.

● Ask the children about the smallest toys they have and the largest places they have been to, such as a beach, a playing field, a sports ground or a cave.

● Discuss how many items they can draw in a tiny space and whether pencil crayons are suitable for the purpose. Can they think of any more suitable drawing tools?

Development Work

- Create a class drawing by asking each child to complete a tiny picture. Cut these out and mount them close together as a collage on a large sheet of paper. If you still have space, repeat the exercise and see how many tiny images are needed to fill the space. When complete, count how many small pictures there are.

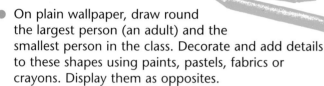

- On plain wallpaper, draw round the largest person (an adult) and the smallest person in the class. Decorate and add details to these shapes using paints, pastels, fabrics or crayons. Display them as opposites.

- Photographers sometimes have old rolls of background paper which they no longer use. If you can get hold of one, staple a huge piece of it (bigger than the children) to a wall and allow the children to make a giant abstract picture using as many different media as possible. Encourage them to stretch to the top of the sheet and bend down to the bottom.

- Read the story, *Jack and the Beanstalk* or any other story about a giant and a small person.

- When the weather is fine but the Sun is safely behind clouds, ask the children to lie down outside and look at the huge sky.

- Observe tiny creatures under large stones.

Display

- Display the matchbox pictures as a group of paintings in a miniature gallery. For the gallery, use a shallow, plain cardboard box or a wooden fruit box. Add a background sheet of paper decorated with tyre prints.

- Offcuts of paper can provide an unusual frame for a single picture. Experiment by framing two or four sides.

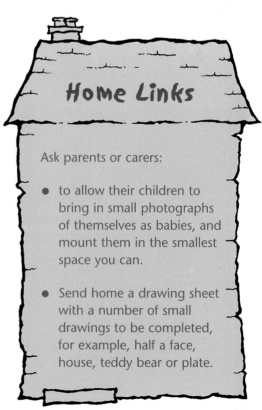

Home Links

Ask parents or carers:

- to allow their children to bring in small photographs of themselves as babies, and mount them in the smallest space you can.

- Send home a drawing sheet with a number of small drawings to be completed, for example, half a face, house, teddy bear or plate.

Making Spaces

Technique

- Make an abstract design on a sheet of white card using strips of masking tape. Try different lengths and positions. Some of the strips could overlap. Press the strips down firmly.

- Using two or three toning colours of felt-tipped pen, colour the whole of the card and masking tape areas. Check there are no white spaces and that the colouring is strong around the edges of the tape.

- Carefully peel off the strips of tape to reveal the crisp, white lines which are now in stark contrast to the colour.

Discussion Points

- Name the colours and talk about filling in the white space as you work using appropriate vocabulary (space, colour, white, leave, gap, fill-in and strip).

- Look at the shapes revealed and ask for each child's opinion of the effect. Do they like it? Was it fun to do?

Development Work

● Use tape and one colour of felt-tipped pen to make a pattern of parallel lines or checks.

● Cut out pumpkin faces from tracing paper and use the masking tape to form the features. Paint over the whole face with autumn colours, such as orange, yellow and brown, then strip off the tape to reveal the features.

● Cut out scary faces from dark coloured paper and form the features with tape. Use chalk to cover the tape and most of the black paper for an indistinct, smoky effect. Strip off the tape to reveal ghostly faces in the dark.

● Look at pictures of masks in books or use plastic toy masks. Look at the spaces for the eyes and mouth.

Display

● Mount the abstracts on a large cardboard box, as shown below. If necessary, cover the box with coloured paper. Stand the box on a table or on the floor for the children to walk around.

● Make a stripy background by rolling paint onto the back of wallpaper. Mount the scary faces on this for a startling effect.

● Fix translucent pumpkin faces to a window or to a bright background. Bend them outward and fix in position to leave a space behind for the light.

Home Links

Ask parents or carers to:

● help their children look for space in the patterns on wallpaper or in other designs around the house.

Backgrounds

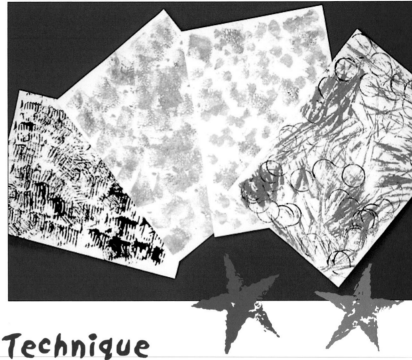

William M

Technique

● Provide various painting 'tools' (such as Cellophane, card tubes, corrugated card strips, toy vehicles and paintbrushes), assorted paper and ready-mix paint.

● To make a background, pick the colour and size of paper required, select one or more of the painting tools and the colour of paint.

● Use the tools by:
  – dabbing brushes into the paint and then onto the paper to make feathery blobs, or paint smooth lines
  – scrunching a handful of Cellophane and dabbing it into a saucer of paint, then dabbing it over the paper
  – using the ends of card tubes to print circles or curves
  – using the uneven side of corrugated card to print stripes
  – running the wheels of small toy vehicles in the paint and then over the paper.

Discussion Points

● Talk about the idea of 'background' as being 'what can be seen behind things that are at the front' (the 'foreground'). Ask a child to stand in front of a wall. Explain that the child is 'in front', nearest to the class, and the wall is 'behind' him or her.

● When working, use appropriate vocabulary (dab, scrunch, roll, wipe, fill, empty and space).

● Discuss what a painted background could represent. Do they think it is a field, the sea, the night sky, or something more nebulous, such as happiness or magic?

Development Work

- Add texture by printing some open shapes or small blobs with PVA glue and then sprinkling glitter, sand, washing powder or sawdust over it.

- Add textured or printed borders, such as bubble prints.

- For a large frieze, paint a background, such as the seaside, with brushes and sponges (used to wipe or dab). Join up the sea, sand and sky. Draw pictures of people, boats, birds and buildings, then cut them out and stick them onto the scene where appropriate.

- Look at a variety of illustrated books with the children and talk about the backgrounds the artists have used. Are they full of detail or are they plain?

- Explain that a picture and its background can be enclosed by a border. Mount a picture on a sheet of white paper, allowing a 2-centimetre border all round. Use wax crayons to draw wavy lines continuously all around this border. (Use several colours that match with those in the picture.)

Display

- Use plain wallpaper as large backing sheets for displays of any type of work. Design a painted background pattern. These could be sponged, printed, or painted on with a roller.

- Use background paintings for displaying notices and labels.

Home Links

Ask parents or carers to:

- look at pictures or photographs with their children and use the words 'background' and 'foreground' to describe where things are.

53

Card Sculptures

Technique

● Provide a wide selection of card cut into rectangles of different sizes, coloured card for the backing, scissors and PVA glue.

● Encourage the children to experiment by arranging the card pieces in various ways before gluing. The rectangles can be leaned against each other in a standing position, stacked or lined up.

● Encourage the children to use scissors to cut thin card pieces to a smaller size if they wish.

● After experimentation, fix the card pieces onto the backing with PVA glue.

Discussion Points

● Encourage the use of appropriate vocabulary when working (rectangle, build, stack, lean, place, position and fix).

● Ask the children: 'What does the sculpture look like when viewed from the side?' 'Which is the best viewpoint?'

● Discuss the texture and colour of the card and what it is like to cut.

● Discuss whether or not it is difficult to build with rectangular, flat shapes.

● Ask the children what they think of the neutral tones of the cardboard. Do they like them?

Development Work

- Make a huge sculpture with rectangles, using items such as old carpet tiles, floor tiles and rush mats. Find a large space and ask the children to help you make the abstract sculpture on the floor.

- Try building a temporary sculpture with PE mats.

- Create a sculpture with cardboard boxes. Encourage the children to make one that is bigger than themselves. Photograph the sculpture with the sculptors standing alongside it.

- Look for naturally occurring sculptures of thin shapes, for example a pile of fallen books, books on a shelf, biscuits in a tin and piles of paving stones.

Display

- Mount two or three sculptures together, placing some fresh green leaves behind one of the sculptures for contrast.

- Concertina-fold a large sheet of card in a contrasting or complementary colour and glue one sculpture onto each fold. Display on a low surface so that the children can look into each fold and see the sculptures from different angles.

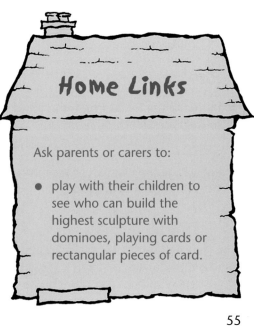

Home Links

Ask parents or carers to:

- play with their children to see who can build the highest sculpture with dominoes, playing cards or rectangular pieces of card.

Sculpture with Tubes

Learning Intentions

- To explore the sculpting possibilities of a single three-dimensional form.

- To use space as part of a sculpture.

Technique

- Provide circular, rectangular and square cork tiles, carpet tiles or pieces of card for the bases of the sculptures. Also provide PVA glue, card tubes of various sizes and assorted small, natural materials, such as shells, seeds and leaves.

- Ask the children to build with the tubes. Encourage them to try a variety of methods:
  - stacking tubes
  - threading a small tube through a larger tube
  - standing thin tubes inside wider tubes
  - placing tubes at right angles to each other
  - placing them in neat rows, upright or lying down.

- Select a tile or piece of card for the base. Using PVA glue sparingly, build the sculpture by attaching the tubes to the base and to other tubes.

- While the sculpture is drying, encourage the children to look into the tubes from all directions.

- Discuss where to put a selection of natural items, for example inside a cavity, on top of a tube, in between two tubes and so on. Help the children to identify the position they choose.

Discussion Points

- Use positional language such as 'through', 'between', 'inside', 'under', 'above', 'on top' and 'below'.

- Discuss what can be seen through the various holes. 'Is the eye led on towards another tube or is there a "blank wall"?' 'Is there a series of tubes or tunnels?'

- Discuss any problems the children encountered when constructing the sculptures.

Display

- Display the sculptures on a wall by mounting a selection on a natural backing board, such as a piece of woven fencing or rush matting. Include one or two twig or leaf decorations.

- Display five sculptures on a cardboard box by gluing each sculpture to each visible face.

- Mount viewing tubes among card-tube sculptures so that the viewer's eye goes in-between the sculptures to see the pictures.

Development Work

- Ask a group of children to make a sculpture without a base. How high or long can the children make it? (If necessary, use a contact adhesive for quicker drying.)

- Visit a park or play area that has concrete tunnels to play in. Alternatively, borrow or buy folding plastic play tunnels so that the children can feel what it is like to be inside a tube like the ones they have been using.

- Make 'viewing tubes' by mounting tiny pictures from old books or magazines onto circles of card. Glue the pictures to the ends of tubes of different lengths to look through.

- Read the passage in which Pooh gets stuck in a rabbit hole, in *Winnie the Pooh* by A A Milne.

- Read and discuss the story *Peepo* by Janet and Allan Ahlberg.

- Link the sculpture with work in Mathematics and talk about the tubes as cylinders. Make a collection of different food containers that are cylindrical.

Home Links

Ask parents or carers to:

- help their children identify cylinders at home, such as food containers, drinking straws, tubes inside cooking foil or delivered carpets

- encourage their children to collect long tubes to make a giant free-standing sculpture.

Free-standing Sculptures

Learning Intentions

- To construct free-standing sculptures from offcuts of wood.

- To work in a group.

- To use scrap materials creatively to build an abstract sculpture.

Technique

- For a wood sculpture, prepare and provide a selection of wood offcuts (various sizes, textures and shapes) rubbing down any big splinters with sandpaper. Leave some rough edges for the children to smooth off. Also supply wood glue and small twigs.

- Encourage each child to experiment with six different pieces of wood, changing their positions until they are satisfied with the arrangement. Dismantle the sculpture carefully and then rebuild, securing it with wood glue. Add small decorative items such as twigs.

- For a recycled sculpture, provide a large assortment of materials, including containers, sheets, threads and tubes.

- During the construction process, encourage the children to check that shapes and lines look good together. Also encourage them to think how disparate surfaces, such as curves and planes, can be joined together.

- When the structure is complete, discuss what colours or any other finishes should be used.

Discussion Points

- Discuss the feel of the wood and scrap materials. 'Are they heavy, light, warm, cold, rough, smooth, flat, wavy?' 'Have they got corners or rounded edges?'

- Discuss how the pieces fit together. 'Are there any that won't stand up, lean or balance in a certain way?'

- Look all round the sculptures. 'Are all the sides interesting?' 'Do you all agree?'

Development Work

- Make a structure using equal-sized pieces of wood or use a single type of scrap to build with. For example, card tubes, cubes or spheres.

- Ask the children to make a tall model or a flat one so that they have a specific design brief.

- Make a wood model of something 'real', such as a boat or an animal.

- Look at a fallen tree trunk and discover the mini-beasts that live there. Discuss the fact that wood is a living material with a life cycle. Talk about recycling and how the children are using recyclable materials or offcuts in their work.

Display

- Use terracotta plant pots as display stands for individual wood sculptures.

- Display unpainted wood sculptures on a wood tone coloured background. Include grasses or wild flowers to add to the natural effect.

- Place scrap material sculptures against a plain background, if possible where light can cast shadows or shine through holes.

- Display a large sculpture on a box at the end of a corridor.

Home Links

Ask parents or carers to:

- help their children fill out an 'I-spy wood' sheet (include about five items, such as a tree, a rotting log, a wooden model, and a wooden item in the house and outdoors)

- take their children out to look at sculptures, for example to a sculpture park, town park or church.

Clay Sculptures

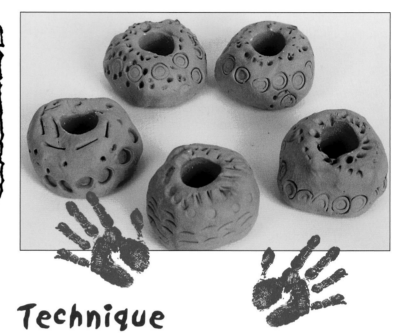

Technique

- Provide self-hardening clay, small rolling pins, modelling tools (plastic knives, forks, spoons, sticks and pencils) and assorted plastic pastry-cutters.

- Place a small bowl of water on the table so that the children can dip the tips of their fingers in to moisten the clay if necessary.

- Make a candleholder using an egg-sized piece of clay. Round the clay with cupped hands, smoothing any creases with a finger. Gently push in a candle to about 1.5 centimetres depth. Leave the candle in and press the clay down on a work surface to flatten the base.

Discussion Points

- Discuss the properties of clay: its texture, temperature, weight, movement and behaviour. Use descriptive vocabulary (damp, sticky, drying, break, crumble, bend, mould, heavy, hard, soft).

- Use working vocabulary (roll, press, bend, squash, smooth, pinch, wet, moisten, cut).

- Talk about the appearance of the damp or dry clay (its colour and dull texture). Can the children think of other things with the same appearance?

- Decorate the candleholder using the clay tools to press, poke, draw or pick at the clay. Enlarge the hole for the candle a little as the clay will shrink slightly as it dries.

- To make clay tiles, roll out an egg-sized piece of clay to a depth of about 1 centimetre. Cut out 10-centimetre square tiles.

- Decorate the tiles using clay tools or add rolled balls or snake-shapes or cut-out motifs. Stick them on by roughening the surface to be joined and adding a dab of water.

Development Work

- Make small pots with balls of clay. Stick the thumb of the writing hand into the clay. Turn the clay ball around, leaving the thumb in as a pivot, and pull outward to widen the hole. (Make sure the thumb is not pushed through the clay base.) Decorate as before.

- Make small animals. Start with an egg-shape and then:
  - for a hedgehog, pull a small nose outwards, add eye-holes with a pencil and prickles by scoring with a fork
  - for a bird, make an oval, squeezing a neck with thumb and first finger. Add indents for eyes and push in a piece of triangular card for a beak. Add clay wings.

- Read the traditional story of *The Gingerbread Man* and make some gingerbread people biscuits, using decorative techniques from the clay work.

- Read stories that tell of festivals of light, such as Christmas, Chinese New Year and Diwali, perhaps reading them by candlelight on a cold, winter's day.

- Display the candleholders in a circular shape to echo their form. Display the sculptures on a low surface so that they can be viewed from above as well as from the sides.

- Create a textured display on a wooden surface with a card backdrop. Stand the clay items on upturned baskets and terracotta pots.

Display

- Make a 'garden face' using strong, brown card as a base. Fix the tiles and candleholders in place with double-sided tape. Use dry leaves for the hair and display upright against a wall.

- Make a totem pole column using a rectangle of coloured card that tones with the clay colour. Fix the tiles along it with double-sided tape.

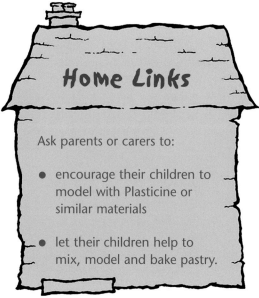

Home Links

Ask parents or carers to:

- encourage their children to model with Plasticine or similar materials

- let their children help to mix, model and bake pastry.

Paper Sculptures

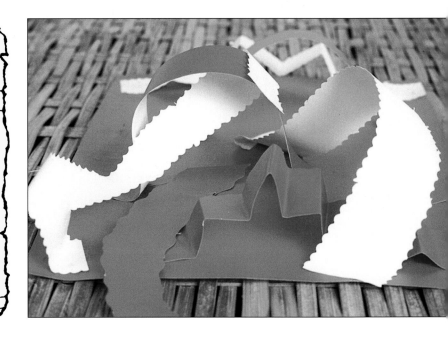

Technique

- Make a paper sculpture using PVA glue and strips and circles of bronze, gold and white paper. Cut a rectangle of bronze paper for the base. Curl strips of paper by tightly winding them around a pencil, concertina-fold rectangles, and fold circles in half. Glue the ends of paper strips to create bridge shapes. Add concertinas, loops, twists and open or closed circles.

- Make a tissue paper sculpture. Cover a sheet of tissue paper with PVA glue, wiping, moulding and squeezing the glue into the paper. Place it on a card base in a rounded, smooth shape. Repeat the process with other colours, placing them next to or round the existing shapes. Finish by placing knotted coils and mounds of other coloured tissues on top.

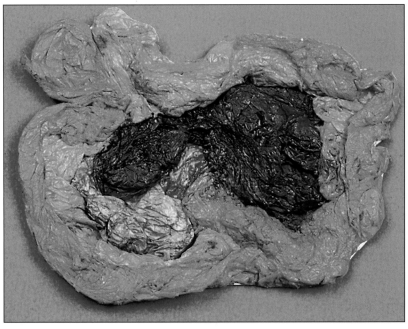

- Use collage skills to make a paper-plate puppet. Experiment with an assortment of materials to find suitable items for the different features of a funny, sad or angry face. Allow the children to cut any materials to size. Glue on the features first and then add hair and perhaps a hat. Glue on a tight roll of paper to the back as a handle (see the photograph on page 63).

- While working on the paper sculptures, discuss how the paper behaves. Can the children recognise that it can be 'bent', 'twisted', 'folded', 'curled', 'threaded', 'looped', 'cut' and 'torn'?

- Look at the paper sculptures from each angle. Discuss the shapes and shadows created.

- While working on the tissue paper sculptures use appropriate vocabulary (twist, floppy, tight, ball, roll, lay, smooth).

- Talk about the intended features on the paper-plate faces (see Development Work). What type of character is to be made? Is it going to look happy, sad, cross, calm, funny? How can the features show this? Use appropriate vocabulary such as 'fix', 'position', 'person' and 'character'.

Development Work

- Make a sculptured face by gluing paper strips and circles to an oval base or a paper plate, for example use folded circles for eyes, a concertina nose, looped ears and curls for hair. Glue the end of a length of dowelling to the back for a handle.

- Make a puppet body from a cone of paper. Cut out a pair of hands or mitten shapes and glue them to the sides of the cone. Push the puppet handle through the top of the cone and secure with glue.

- Make up names and persona for the puppets. Develop a short storyline and let the children speak for their puppet.

- Make a collection of pop-out books with paper sculpture inserts.

- Use the paper-tissue technique to mould names. Form the tissue into ropes and help the children to bend them into the letter shapes.

- Read the story *Hansel and Gretel* and make tissue-paper sculptures of sweets to put on the witch's house.

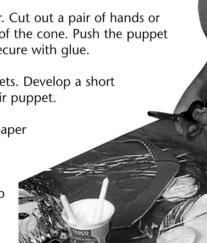

Display

- Fix a tall card tube from the inside of a carpet roll to a wall. Glue the paper strip sculptures in a staggered arrangement around and along it like a totem pole.

- Display a small selection of tissue-paper sculptures in linear form on plain white paper with a brighter background. Pick a colour from each sculpture and make matching top and bottom zigzag borders.

- Display tissue-paper name sculptures at eye level on a bright backing so that children can trace over the letters with their fingers.

- Stand the paper-plate puppets in upturned clay plant pots.

- Make a theatre backdrop with crêpe paper curtains stapled to a backing paper and an art-paper arch. Clothe the puppets with square scarves, then staple them into different poses, stretching out the corners of the scarves for arms.

- Use a textured contrasting background, such matting, to display the paper strip sculptures.

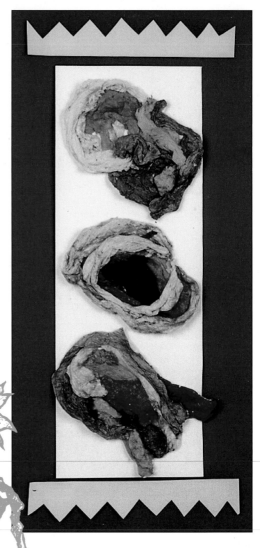

Home Links

Ask parents or carers to:

- help their children to make a simple folded fan from a sheet of paper and to encourage their children to decorate the folds with felt-tipped pens

- help their children to make a glove puppet using a large sock as a base and scraps of material, such as wool and milk-bottle tops for the features.